Leeds
Past

at heart ♡ publications

First Published in 2007 by:
At Heart Ltd, 32 Stamford Street, Altrincham,
Cheshire, WA14 1EY.

in conjunction with

The Yorkshire Evening Post
PO Box 168 Wellington Street
Leeds
LS1 1RF

ISBN: 978-1-84547-131-6
Printed by Bell & Bain, Scotland.

Contents

Introduction

Leeds, the "entrepreneur city" of West Yorkshire, thanks in some measure to its geographic location, has had an energy and vigor which have been its distinguishing characteristics.

In these pages of archive photographs from the *Yorkshire Evening Post* and the *Yorkshire Post* the industrial and commercial hub of a busy, productive region can be seen.

Leeds and the surrounding area have adapted to the changes – some to be welcomed and some to be regretted – which were brought by the advancing 20th Century, and local events in those years which stand out in the area's history are also featured in these pages.

We hope you enjoy this glimpse into Leeds pictorial past.

1930s-1950s

■ Queen's Hotel under construction on January 6, 1937.

■ Alwoodley Motors
Ltd. garage and
Sandmoor Golf Course
in February 11, 1937.

■ The Civic Hall on
September 29, 1937.

■ The River Aire on January 27, 1948, looking from Crown Point Bridge.

■ The river below Crown Point, February 1948.

■ A barge on the
Leeds-Liverpool Canal.

■ Albion Street Stock
Exchange, February 13,
1948.

■ The No.3 Harehills tram picks up passengers in Briggate, September 28, 1948.

■ River Aire at Leeds Bridge, March 1952.

■ The Headrow and a soft-top Standard 8 at the kerb on February 10, 1949.

■ River Aire coal barge on the Leeds-Liverpool Canal. The River Aire can be seen on the left. October 4, 1951.

■ An overturned tram on a snowy day outside Leeds University. February 1951.

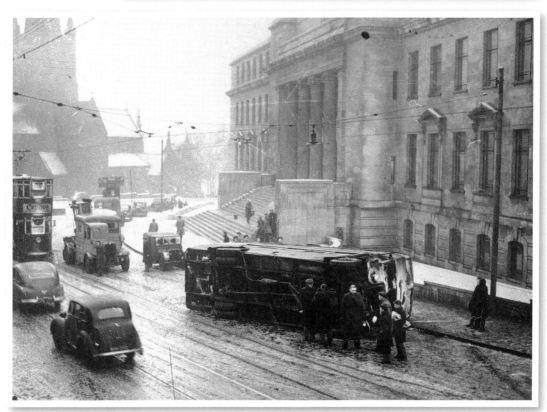

■ After luncheon at Harewood House, the Queen and the Duke of Edinburgh posed with some of the members of the house party. Front row left to right: The Earl of Harewood, the Duke of Edinburgh, the Queen, the Princess Royal, the Hon. Gerald Lascelles. Back row: The Countess of Harewood, Prince and Princess Louis of Hesse and Mrs. Gerald lascelles. October 18, 1958.

■ A Royal smile for Mr. Arthur Tobbell, aged 90, during the Queen's visit to the Brackenhurst Hostel for Aged People on Harrogate Road. October 17, 1958.

■ The Queen with Duke Ellington in Leeds, 1958.

■ Royal visit to Montaque Burtons, Leeds in the 1950s.

■ Princess Margaret on a visit to St. James's Hospital, Leeds in 1954.

■ Leeds Boys' Brigade, May 22, 1958. The Duke of Edinburgh chats with members of a drill squad formed by the 8th Leeds Company of the Boys' Brigade at Burley Methodist Church, including Mr. E. L. Peck, captain of the company.

■ Crowds relax in Roundhay Park, on Whit Sunday, in 1955.

■ Skating on the lake at
Roundhay Park, in 1952.

■ Heat wave scene in Civic Hall gardens, Leeds, May 1952.

■ Mrs.D. Johnstone and Miss B. Wormald, clerks employed at the showrooms of Appleyard of Leeds Ltd. are burning 20,000 gallons of petrol – on paper – on May 26, 1950. The coupons and correspondence were associated with petrol rationing.

■ Spinning wheels, Miss Drusilla Brook (16) of Headingley, Leeds and Mrs. Dorothy Russell (25) of Horsforth on October 17, 1952.

■ Roundhay Park
Swimming Pool 'Lido'
on June 30, 1953.

■ Albion Street, October 19, 1959. Hundreds of people queued in Albion Street, Leeds, in an attempt to book for the following year's holidays.

■ Leeds University's Hall of Residence at Weetwood Lane, Leeds, was for women only in June 1958.

■ Sweeping up the leaves on Mansion Lane, Roundhay, September 21, 1959.

■ A dismal August Bank Holiday scene in Commercial Street, Leeds, as the thunderstorm raged. August 6, 1957.

■ Members in the well-appointed lounge of the YWCA Central Club, May 30, 1957.

■ Commercial Street, November 17, 1952.

■ A typical cell at Armley Jail, Leeds, June 24, 1957. Only one prisoner lived in this cell and he had done his best to add some brightness – a model ship and some birthday cards stand on the table.

■ Leeds (Armley Park) Municipal Golf Course with Kirkstall Power Station beyond, on April 15, 1950.

■ Daffodils on a railway banking, with the bus station and Quarry Hill flats in the background. This photo was taken in 1957.

■ Leeds Children's Day Queen and her attendants, pictured in 1952. From left: Rosemary Stratford, Terry Wilson, Vivienne Howe, John Peniston (crown bearer), Nita Lowther (Children's Day Queen), Brenda Hirst, Tony Wilson and Jean Clough.

■ Rows of cars parked on the site between Eastgate and Union Street, looking from Harewood Street, on February 24, 1959.

■ Street gamblers of York Road, Leeds, in 1955.

■ Fleet of fire appliances lined up outside Gipton Fire Station, Leeds, May 21, 1954.

■ "Slum clearance" in Granville Street, off Beckett Street, Leeds, in 1957.

■ The Shaftesbury Cinema, York Road, Leeds, pictured in 1958.

■ The Tower Picture House c.1950.

■ Leeds City Varieties: in 1953 the BBC recorded a history of the music hall from the Victorian era up to the 1950s.

■ The Scala Ballroom, opened in 1922, and pictured here in May 1957.

■ Theatre Royal on April 1, 1957. Crowds, celebrities, gaiety and regrets marked the last performance on this Saturday night at Leeds Theatre Royal, Hunslet Lane, Leeds. On stage singing a chorus with the cast of the pantomime *'Queen of Hearts'* are Margery Manners, Wilfred and Mable Pickles and Barney Colehan.

■ Leeds tram No. 65 on Boar Lane, photographed in the 1950s.

■ Dismantling the stage at the Theatre Royal
after the last night of performances.

■ Steam locomotive at Leeds in 1958.

■ The 60123 "H.A.Ivatt " 'A1' Pacific at Leeds Central Station, October 16, 1951.

■ Quarry Hill flats and Leeds Bus Station, on April 13, 1954.

■ The beautiful Victorian Queens Arcade on June 24, 1959.

■ An aerial view of Leeds University in August 1953.

■ Old property in Vicar Lane to be demolished, our photo was taken in February 1958.

■ "Permanent House" in the Headrow, as it was in the 1950s.

■ Central Bus Station and Eastgate from the Quarry Hill Flats, October 26, 1956.

■ City Square from station approach. The fine building on the corner of Park Row and Infirmary Street was demolished and replaced by an inferior tower office block, which in turn was demolished and replaced by a building more in keeping with the earlier one. Our photo was taken on August 9, 1956.

■ City Square, May 17, 1957. The blackened building beside Mill Hill Unitarian Chapel was gone within a few years after our picture was taken.

■ Tramlines in Vicar Lane and the
blackened Corn Exchange in the
background, June 1959.

■ A bustling Christmas scene on New
Briggate, December 22, 1951.

■ Junction of
Woodhouse Lane and
Cookridge Street. June
1958.

■ Boar Lane,
Bishopgate, in the late
1950s.

■ Boar Lane in June 1957.

■ Bond Street on August 9, 1956.

■ Looking down Briggate on a Saturday afternoon, December 22, 1951.

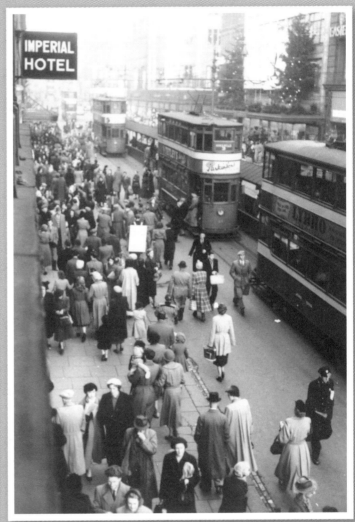

■ Christmas shoppers in Leeds, Briggate. December 1953.

■ An evening scene
on Briggate in
February 1957.

■ The Saturday before Christmas, shoppers on Briggate, December 22, 1951.

■ Briggate on May 24, 1957.

■ Looking down Park Row towards City Square, Leeds. August 31, 1956.

1960s

■ Rowing boats moored on the lakeside at Roundhay Park in August 1964.

■ Sledging at Roundhay Park in January 1962.

■ View from Communications Tower at Cookridge in September 1966. Much more of the landscape in this view would be covered by housing over the next few decades.

■ Leeds University extensions, June 1960.

■ Leeds rail accident August 11, 1961. Repair work on a damaged parapet at the scene of the crash. The line had already been reopened. Note the motor vehicles below the parapet that were damaged by falling masonry.

■ Albert Johanneson signs for Leeds Utd with Gerry Francis, and Don Revie in 1961. Between this date and 1970, he made 200 appearances for United, scoring 68 goals. Johanneson was the first black footballer to play in the FA Cup final when Leeds met Liverpool in 1965.

■ Albion Place, Leeds, April 14, 1964. The Oxfam shop was opened on this day by Sir Roger Stevens, Vice-Chancellor of Leeds University.

■ This is the decorated centre of Leeds Prison, Armley, in December 20, 1963. In the centre is the Christmas tree, hung with make-believe parcels. Bare lamp bulbs are covered with cardboard lanterns.

■ Middleton Broom Colliery, Belle Isle, Leeds, closed in 1968 and later demolished. Our picture was taken on June 4, 1969.

■ Members of Leeds City Police Mounted Division riding along the Headrow, Leeds. June 1967.

■ The third of three microwave radio transmission aerials for the provision of telephone trunk services was hoisted into position on Tinshill Tower, Cookridge, Leeds, in 1967.

■ Greystone Street area off Kirkstall Road 1961. Councillor Mrs. May Sexton (in centre, wearing dark costume) talked to members of Leeds City Council and local residents. Immediately to the left of Councillor Sexton is Councillor Miss Aimee Tong, wearing a floral patterned dress.

■ Midland Bank, Craven Dairies, Judsons and Brill are among some of the businesses occupying the handsome terrace (since demolished) in Belgrave Street, which came off Wade Lane and ran parallel with Merrion Street, Leeds, April 22, 1967.

■ Bischoff's House, Leeds, a fine example of a Queen Anne house, it was the sole survivor of the 15 city merchants' houses illustrated on the earliest known map of Leeds of 1725, and was finally demolished in the 1960s.

■ Boar Lane, Leeds, October 8, 1963.

■ Debris and litter, described as 'A disgrace to Leeds'. York Road, All Saints Street, Leeds. December 11, 1965.

■ A Ford Anglia with its distinctive racked-back rear window heads across the new box junction at the Headrow-Vicar Lane crossing, on October 21, 1968. Nearly three decades later many motorists still have no idea what box junctions are for.

■ Briggate. November 13, 1967.

■ The hideous new traffic signal gantry across Briggate. June 10, 1968.

■ A Hillman passes an MG TD, a Mini and a Mini van in a customarily crowded Clarendon Place, near Leeds University, May 7, 1968.

■ Mrs Tilly Bullough sees children safely across the junction of Main Street and Church Lane, Garforth on July 12, 1965.

■ Harehills, Leeds 1967.

■ Christmas shoppers laden with the fruits of battle queue in Briggate for the bus home on December 24, 1962.

■ The Headrow, January 6, 1969. Pedestrians wait to cross at the junction of Eastgate, the Headrow and Vicar Lane.

■ A display of curtain fabrics at bargain prices in one of the windows of Thom's Household Stores. King Edward Street, Leeds, April 2, 1968.

■ Long queues of people wait for buses, which were reduced by the overtime ban, at the junction of The Calls and Vicar Lane, Leeds. October 23, 1967.

■ The RAC's Yorkshire Headquarters in Regent Street, Leeds, 1960. The car parked outside is an Armstrong Siddley Sapphire, sometimes referred to as the "poor man's Rolls-Royce".

■ A queue on the A1, south of Wetherby, at the junction with the Leeds Road, which carried a line of cars right back to Collingham. April 10, 1966.

■ Minis from this time are still seen in their original form, while all the other marques in this picture are rarities. Great George Street, Leeds, October 17, 1967.

■ Briggate, Leeds, on October 7, 1967.

■ King Edward Hotel, King Edward Street, Leeds, February 14, 1964.

■ Merrion Centre, Leeds, in the 1960s.

■ This picture shows new pedestrian underpass.

■ The picture shows 'Mood scene' in 1964 at the Mecca Ballroom, Merrion Centre, Leeds.

■ A multi-storey office block at the Merrion Centre, Leeds. February 21, 1966.

■ The first Piazza in Leeds takes shape between Russell Street and Bond Street. November 27, 1967.

■ The opening of Leeds International Pool 1967. It was designed by John Poulson Architects who were based in Pontefract (Poulson was later jailed, but not for designing this), it was discovered, too late, that the swimming lanes were not wide enough for the pool to qualify as an Olympic-sized pool.

■ An up-to-the-minute office block in East Parade, seen from King Street, on March 5, 1967. In a few years' time, it would appear very dated.

■ One of the most distinctive office blocks in Leeds, until the 1990s when it was demolished and few regretted its passing.

■ The bold design of the new Guiseley Swimming Baths. April 24, 1967.

■ The new Silver Blades Ice Rink, Kirkstall Road, Leeds. April 1962.

■ Multi-storey flats contrast with earlier buildings in our picture taken in 1964. The wholesale demolition of back-to-back houses came to an abrupt end in the 1980s when it was realised, that with some modifications, they had a perfectly viable future.

■ View from Westgate along the Headrow, dominated by the still-blackened Town Hall.

■ Whitelock's pub, Leeds, 1966.

■ Dodsworth Court which connects Trinity Street and Briggate, Leeds. September 19, 1968.

■ The Bar at the Varieties on
November 14, 1963.

■ Leeds City
Varieties in 1968.

■ Headingley alleyway in 1967. "Concrete lamp standards are now replacing the old gas lamps in this picturesque narrow alleyway, just over a mile from Leeds City Centre. Running from Cumberland Road to Grosvenor Road, Headingley, it is only about four feet wide. It runs alongside the University of Leeds Agricultural Department Experimental Gardens."

■ The "Castle" folly in Roundhay Park in the 1960s.

■ Inside the Corn Exchange, 1966, when it was still a corn exchange. These are the sample tables which the traders used, the samples being laid out in the cavity which is exposed when the desk top is raised and becomes a counter.

■ Coming up to a quarter to three in the Corn Exchange, 1966.

■ The Corn Exchange when it was still blackened like all the other city-centre buildings in Leeds.

■ The Bank of England, Leeds, 1966.

■ Victoria Quarter County Arcade, 1968 – evidence that some things have improved.

■ Thornton's Arcade, October 7, 1968.

■ Dark Arches, January 19, 1968. "Deep within the Dark Arches, part of the system by which 10 acres of Leeds City Station (formerly the New Station and the Wellington Station) were built over the River Aire".

■ The facade of the Queen's Hotel in the final stages of being cleaned.

■ The imposing Forum Cinema in Chapeltown. April 1960.

■ Happy memories for some...the Shaftesbury Cinema, York Road, Leeds, pictured in 1964.

■ The Tatler Cinema on Boar Lane, pictured in the 1960s.

■ Empire Theatre, February 23, 1961 and the audience applauds at the Empire for the last time.

■ The Empire Theatre on February 25, 1961. "Today's picture of the front of the Leeds Empire, which closes after the last show tonight. The site is to become a shopping arcade".

■ The inside of the Empire Theatre, the biggest building of the Edwardian redevelopment between Briggate and Vicar Lane. The entrance was in Briggate and the theatre seated 2,500. The theatre finally closed in 1961.

■ Isaac Robson and Co. Ltd., new premises in Wortley, Moor Lane, Leeds, 1964. Kango hammers being serviced in the repair and maintenance department.

■ Leeds tannery, Kitchin and Co. Ltd on September 29, 1964. "Shaving the reduction of the hide grain to a level thickness, is a precision operation in the production of leather."

■ Whiteley Ltd, Leeds, paper makers on September 19, 1963. "Crane operator Jim Gill casts an eye on 1,000 tons of raw material in the rag house. Here the cotton, much of it discarded overalls and cotton clippings, is chopped finely to begin the process of transformation into paper and board".

■ Cross Green wholesale fruit and vegetable market in Leeds, October 17, 1966.

■ Leeds and Bradford Airport in the 1960s.

■ Bradford Airport in 1968. The control tower, the nerve centre at Yeadon.

■ Leeds General Infirmary Casualty waiting room, 1967.

■ Leeds General Infirmary in 1966. This man is measuring the amount of noise generated, despite the appeal for quietness outside the Brotherton Wing of Leeds Infirmary.

■ Leeds Boys' Brigade, September 3, 1960. "Representative detachments of the Yorkshire District of the Boys' Brigade marched past Leeds Town Hall. Salute taken by the Brigade president, Lord Maclay".

1970s

■ An aerial view of the extensive damage caused by the fire at Kirkgate Market, Leeds. This picture was taken on December 15, 1975.

■ Firefighters tackle a blaze in York Place in the heart of the city on January 3, 1972.

■ A fire on May 21, 1974 in the County Shopping Centre in County Arcade.

■ Thornton's Arcade, July 20, 1976. The caption with this photo read: "Famous figures on the arcade clock they may be, but Charlie Farrar's family have been around to look after them ever since they arrived nearly a century ago".

■ March 11, 1974. Barry Birdsall has a pint at the Newlands Hotel, Hyde Park Road, Leeds, after becoming the first Leeds streaker.

■ Park Square, August 30, 1979. Hundreds of people turned up at the Leeds Immunisation Centre for cholera jabs after an outbreak in Spain.

■ Meter attendant Mrs. Eleanor Greenwood signals "no entry" to Commercial Street because of flying debris during a gale on November 23, 1973.

■ Boar Lane, September 24, 1974. A covered walkway was taking shape behind the untidy scaffolding on the left.

■ Both here and on the opposite page are photographs of Briggate on September 16, 1972. Not quite the pedestrian-friendly thoroughfare it would later become but these benches and floral displays suggested how things might develop.

■ Pedestrians crossing
Briggate on December
5, 1971.

■ Briggate at night,
April 9, 1971.

■ The Headrow seen from Marlborough flats on September 9, 1970.

■ Grid lock on the Headrow, September 25, 1970.

■ Cardigan Grove, Burley, demolished in 1970. The picture shows Mrs Ethel Kay the last resident of the street.

■ The Leeds Permanent headquarters on the left, seen on June 14, 1971. This would eventually be transformed into a hotel and restaurant, and The Light precinct.

■ September 10, 1970 and back-to-backs on and around Burley Road, which survived the earlier zeal to pull all such houses down.

■ The Rex, Cinema, February 1976.

■ The Merrion Centre as it looked in 1978.

■ A rag and bone man with a pram, instead of a horse and cart, working Chapeltown in 1980.

■ Rag and bone men on their rounds in Little London on December 30, 1970.

■ The famous Cottage Road Cinema, in Headingley, in 1976.

■ Leeds and residents demonstrate at a pedestrian crossing on Scott Hall Road, Chapel Allerton, in the 1970s. Then, as now, speeding drivers are heartily disliked by those living on urban busy roads.

■ Leeds Bus Station, as it was in August 18, 1977, when opposite the station was the vast Quarry Hill flats complex.

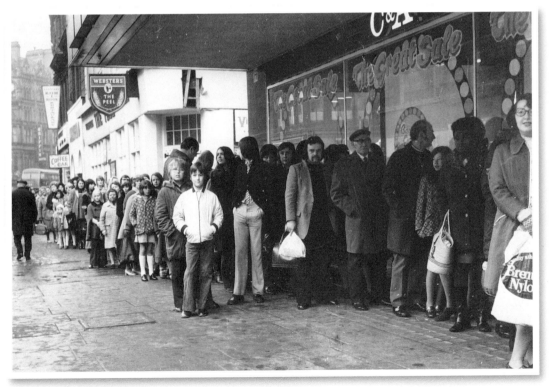

■ Queuing for the C&A New Year sales on January 1, 1973.

■ Motorists dig out their vehicles in York Road after a snow fall on February 14, 1979.

■ Part of a long queue for the New Year sale at Schofields store on the Headrow, on January 3, 1976.

■ Drivers who had been forced to abandon their vehicles trudge down a slip road, February 14, 1979.

■ Mrs. Beryl Davies sees children safely across Otley Road, outside the Richmond House and Far Headingley Preparatory School, in June 1975.

■ Showing community spirit unemployed youngsters work on a landscaping project in Leeds, November 6, 1978.